PLAY BETTER GOLF

POWER DRIVING

Swing on the right track

Beverly Lewis

Illustrations by Ken Lewis

TIGER BOOKS INTERNATIONAL
LONDON

3151
This edition published in 1992 by
Tiger Books International PLC, London
© 1991 Colour Library Books Ltd, Godalming, Surrey
Printed and bound in Singapore
ISBN 1-85501-223-5

Contents

Beverly and Ken Lewis

Beverly Lewis became a professional golfer in 1978 and has twice been Chairman of the Women's Professional Golf Association. A PGA qualified professional since 1982, she has played in many major tournaments and is an experienced teacher. She has been a regular contributor to *Golf World* magazine in the United Kingdom for six years and is the only woman on their teaching panel. She has won two tournaments on the WPGA circuit but now concentrates on her teaching commitments.

Beverly is co-author of *Improve Your Golf* (published in the UK by Collins Willow, revised edition), and has written the other titles in the *Golf Clinic Series*. Her interests include music and playing the organ.

Ken Lewis trained at the Southend College of Art and then worked as a commercial artist. He has illustrated many golf books, working with players such as Peter Alliss, Alex Hay and Sandy Lyle. His projects include illustrating newspaper instructional features and strips by Greg Norman and Nick Faldo, and he works for *Golf* Magazine in the United States. His hobbies include building and flying his own aeroplane.

Introduction

Having played golf more years than I care to remember, the early days of discovering what to me was 'the secret', are a distant memory. I played golf for far too long before reading any book that clearly set out the basic fundamentals that even the most raw beginner could master. In *Power Driving*, the first book in the 'Golf Clinic' series, I have outlined the most important points you must work on and develop in order to achieve your maximum potential. Based on many years' teaching, and playing the game at professional tournament level, I have highlighted the easiest way to play golf well and consistently. I have also tried to pinpoint the most likely faults that will occur at any time in the swing. However, this book does not set out to cure your slice or hook – that comes in a later edition in the series – but if you work on the advice in these pages, then you should start to improve automatically, whatever your fault.

I have written the book for both men and women. Although we may have different levels of strength, I believe that we should try to play golf using the same principles. Having played so in many Pro-Ams with men, I can state categorically that they feel that they can relate to a woman professional more than a man, since women tend to hit the ball approximately the same distance as them. They usually, quite generously, acknowledge that a woman professional's smooth effortless swing serves as a good reminder of what they should be trying to achieve.

I hope you enjoy the book and find something within it that will improve your golf, no matter what your standard.

CHAPTER ONE

What are we trying to achieve?

There is a saying in golf: 'drive for show, and putt for dough'. Now while there may be more than a grain of truth in that adage, there is little chance of putting for too much dough, i.e. money, if driving is the weak part of your game. Naturally, even among the best players in the world, there are those renowned for their driving skills, and others who are better known as superb putters, but you cannot expect to achieve your best scores if the first shot on each hole lands in the rough, a bunker, lake or forest. The best putter in the world is going to be hard pressed to salvage a decent score.

Anyone who has been to a professional golf tournament will undoubtedly have been impressed by the standard of driving – not only the power but also the accuracy. Time and time again, the top professionals' super-smooth swings

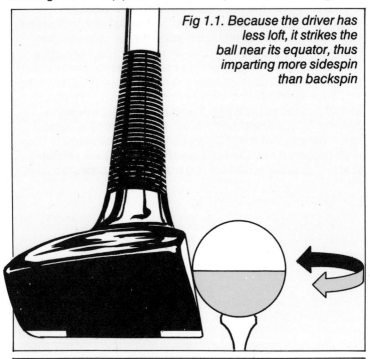

Fig 1.1. Because the driver has less loft, it strikes the ball near its equator, thus imparting more sidespin than backspin

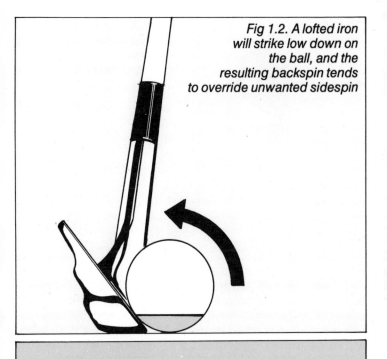

Fig 1.2. A lofted iron will strike low down on the ball, and the resulting backspin tends to override unwanted sidespin

produce shots that seem to explode off the clubface and travel hundreds of yards to the optimum point in the fairway. To be able to reproduce shots of such high quality is probably every club golfer's dream, and in writing this book I have tried to highlight the most important factors that permit professionals to achieve these exhilarating shots, and hope that by integrating them into your game you will start to emulate the skills of your heroes or, indeed, heroines.

The drive that is struck powerfully from the middle of the clubface to the middle of the fairway, is not only extremely satisfying, but sets up a possible birdie chance and makes par much more of a formality.

But why is it that this department of the game can cause such misery to many players, who, although they may not be very low handicap golfers, are able to hit a high proportion of their other shots to an acceptable standard? Well, the problem arises with a driver mainly because of its lack of loft on the clubface, and it is this factor that accentuates any flaws in the swing. When using other clubs, the additional loft will tend to offset these imperfections to a

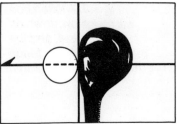

Fig 1.3. At impact, the clubhead should be swinging directly towards the target, with the club face square to the target

Fig 1.4. The clubhead should approach the ball on a shallow arc

certain extent, and you are able to proceed around the golf course in a fairly direct manner. The driver, due to its straight face, strikes the ball on its equator, and thus any hint of sidespin is emphasised (Fig 1.1). A more lofted club will strike the ball lower down, and create more backspin which, to a certain extent, tends to balance unwanted sidespin (Fig 1.2). Do not ignore the fact that the driver has the longest shaft of all the clubs, and this can seem rather unwieldy, and therefore harder to swing in a controlled manner. And control does seem to desert many players when they take the driver in their hands. When using their irons, if a 6 iron will not hit the ball far enough, they quite happily take a 5 iron for the shot, knowing that there is a limit to how far they can hit each iron. However, when it comes to the driver, many golfers seem to think that infinity is their limit. They thrash away with the club, hoping beyond all reality that they will suddenly be able to hit the ball an additional 50 yards if they launch everything into the shot. What does happen is that any hint of smoothness and good timing disappear, and the ball goes nowhere.

Poor driving can send you scurrying to unchartered parts of the course and totally ruin your round, but improve this department of your game and who knows how low your handicap may become. To produce a long straight drive:

▶ at impact the clubhead must be travelling at speed directly towards the target;

▶ the clubface must be at right angles to this path;

▶ it must be travelling at a shallow angle of attack (Figs 1.3 & 1.4);

▶ the ball must be struck from the middle of the clubface.

To produce this set of circumstances, the swing-path has to be from in-to straight to-in. Now if the implications of that statement are not totally clear, let me explain further, using the clock face to give you a better picture of the situation.

Imagine that as you address the ball, it is in the centre of a clock face. You are standing at 6 o'clock, with 3 o'clock on your right, and 9 o'clock on your left (Fig 1.5). As you swing the clubhead away from the ball, for a short distance it will travel towards 3 o'clock. Then, as your body continues to turn, so the clubhead will leave that straight line and start to swing inwards and upwards between 3 and 4 o'clock. Ideally you will then swing it down again on a similar line, strike the ball while the clubhead is travelling directly towards the target at 9 o'clock, and then, as the body continues its turn, the clubhead will start to swing inwards to 8 o'clock.

Throughout the book I will refer to this clock face system of describing the clubhead swing-path, since not only is it an easy system from an instructional point of view but it is also a simple method of analysis that you can take onto the course to help during your round.

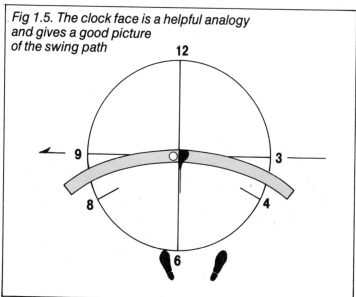

Fig 1.5. The clock face is a helpful analogy and gives a good picture of the swing path

CHAPTER TWO

The right equipment

Before I explain any more about the swing, I think that a few points about equipment would be helpful. Many people believe that you cannot go into the professional's shop and 'buy' success, but you can buy and use equipment that can either help or hinder your game, and this is never truer than with the driver.

The driver face

There are several aspects to consider when choosing a driver, and one of the most important is the amount of loft on the club. As I have already pointed out, the less loft on a club, the more it will impart sidespin – wanted or not – on the ball. So if you are someone who viciously hooks or slices the ball, you should choose a driver with plenty of loft. The better the player you become, the more able you will be to

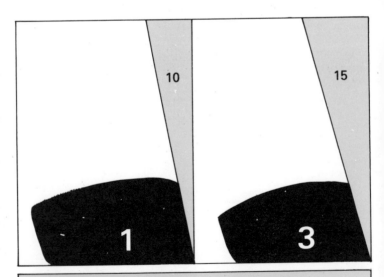

Fig 2.1. The higher numbered woods have more degrees of loft and can help to hit the ball with less sidespin, and therefore straighter

use a club that is relatively straight-faced, and thus benefit from the extra distance that can be gained from such a club. So how should you select the right loft? Most drivers will have a loft of between about 9 and 12 degrees, and it is one that is 12 degrees that is the easier to hit. If your driver is straight-faced, it is better to use the more lofted 3 or 4 wood in the set, until such time that you can hit reliably (Fig 2.1). Your driver will gain you maybe 10 to 15 yards, but that is no use if it sends the ball too far off line – better to sacrifice distance for accuracy.

A deep faced driver is also more difficult to use, so check that aspect of the club as well, since if it is deeper than one-and-three-quarter inches it will be difficult to use. If you hook the ball, you may find that a slightly open faced club would help to hit the ball straighter (Fig 2.2), whereas the player who slices the ball consistently, would be better suited to one that sits a little closed (Fig 2.3). Do not expect to be able to judge these angles and lofts with an untrained eye, so always ask your professional for advice. He (or she) might ask you to hit a few shots and will help in your final choice.

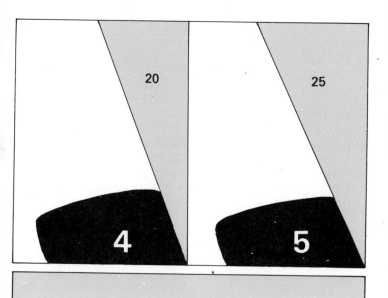

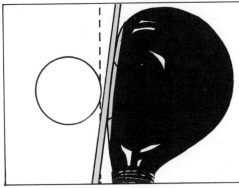

Fig 2.2. The player who hooks could benefit from a driver that sits open

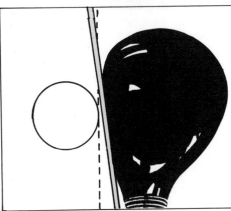

Fig 2.3. The player who slices could benefit from a driver that sits closed

The shaft

Most men should use a driver with a man's regular shaft. It is only the stronger player, who hits the ball a long way and tends to draw or hook the ball consistently, who might benefit from a stiffer shaft. Alternatively, I know many men who, accepting that they are not as strong as they used to be, get on better and gain some length by using lighter whippier ladies' clubs. Most ladies should use ladies' clubs (often they inherit their husbands' cast-offs, which are totally unsuitable). It is only those who are stronger than average who should be considering a man's driver. Since men's clubs are longer, they are generally heavier to swing, and if you are not sufficiently strong to control that extra weight and to cope with the stiffer shaft, then there is no benefit from the club.

12

Swing-weight	C0-C5	C6-C8	C9-D2	D3-D5
Shaft	L	L or R	R	S or XS
Category of Player	Lady beginner and average lady player. Slow swing and hand action.	Strong lady and weaker man. Reasonable hand and club speed. Man may feel that a lighter club is easier to control and L shaft helps clubhead speed.	Strong lady and average man. Good hand action and clubhead speed.	Strong man. Very fast hand action and clubhead speed.

Fig 2.4. This table shows which swing weight and shaft flex suit the different categories of golfers

The swing weight

Along with the various flexes of shaft to consider, you must also select a club that is the correct swing weight for you. Swing weight is a system of measuring the balance of a club, and it also helps to indicate how heavy a club feels when it is swung. The scale starts at the light end for ladies, which is anything from C0 to C9, continuing into the men's range which overlaps the ladies' heavier club in the C8 to C9 category up to D5 and onwards at the heaviest end (Fig 2.4).

A man's average driver could be at the light end of the scale D0, progressing to D2 as a medium weight, with D4 onwards being considered quite heavy. Some professionals, since they create very fast clubhead speed, can use clubs that would register about D5 or D6, but they would also use a stiff, or very stiff shafted, club to control this extra weight. However, they are exceptional and most men would be best suited to a club that will not feel too heavy to swing when they are nearing the end of a round and beginning to feel tired. The less athletic woman may find a club of around C3 most suitable, whereas a stonger player, perhaps someone who has excelled in other sports, may find that this weight of club is like a wand in her hand. She would need a heavier club in the ladies' range, or maybe discover that a men's lightweight club suits her better. In recent years, there have been many more lightweight clubs on the market, and for the stronger woman, or weaker man, these can prove ideal.

The lie

The lie of the club is the angle between the shaft and the base, or sole, of the club. When buying a set of irons, this is one of the most important aspects to consider, since a club with an incorrect lie can affect the shot. However, when using a driver the ball is on a tee peg, so the lie is not so important. But if, for instance, you are five foot tall, and use a man's length driver, make sure that the lie is not too upright.

Grip thickness

One further point to consider is the thickness of the grip. Ideally, when the left hand is closed around the handle, the last three fingers should be quite close to the base of the thumb (Fig 2.5). Too great a gap will probably deny you enough hand action and control. Alternatively, grips that are too thin may not allow the club to sit snugly in your left hand

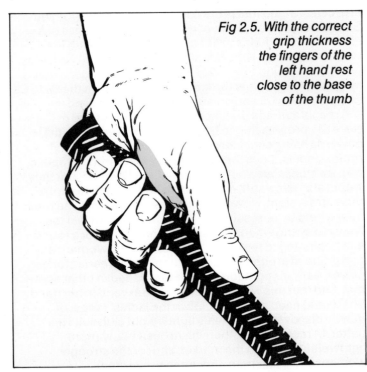

Fig 2.5. With the correct grip thickness the fingers of the left hand rest close to the base of the thumb

and then one of two things may happen: you might grip the club just in the fingers of this hand, instead of the palm and fingers; or, trying to place the club correctly across the palm, you will find the fingers tending to 'run into' the base of the left thumb, preventing a solid grip. Remember, however, that if you change the grip thickness on your clubs, a thinner grip will make the club feel heavier to swing whereas thicker grips will lighten it. Thinner grips will also encourage more hand action, while thicker ones will have the reverse affect.

Consult the expert

I am sure that your local professional will be only too pleased to help you choose a driver, but you should always tell him your handicap and the characteristics of your game. Ideally, he can watch you hit a few shots, and then he can better assess the right club. These days we are spoilt for choice, with drivers now being made not only in wood but also in carbon and metal, and with either carbon or metal shafts, so you can see why you should seek professional advice.

Summary

So to summarize club choice, the most important factors are the loft, how the face lies, the shaft flex, swing weight and grip thickness. It takes some professionals years to find exactly the right driver, and when they have done so, they guard it with their lives. So do not be too hasty in buying the first one you see – ask your professional what will suit your ability, and go from there.

CHAPTER THREE

The importance of the correct grip

If you look at the best players in the world, it is obvious that they do not all grip the club in exactly the same way. Their different styles of playing are best suited by the grip that they use. However, among the vast majority of these golfers, both men and women, certain fundamentals are common. In other words, although their grips may vary slightly, they do conform within certain boundaries. Take a look at a group of club golfers at any driving range or practice ground, and unfortunately I can guarantee that the majority will be gripping the club in such a way that producing consistently good golf shots will be very difficult.

So often, when people start to play golf, they grip the club in a manner that feels most comfortable, but which, in most cases, will not produce powerful shots. Sound foundations are necessary in order to achieve your maximum potential in golf and build a powerful, reliable swing. The grip is mainly responsible for the clubface alignment and, as I have already stated, when using the driver, if you do not have the clubface square at impact, the ball is going to curve more

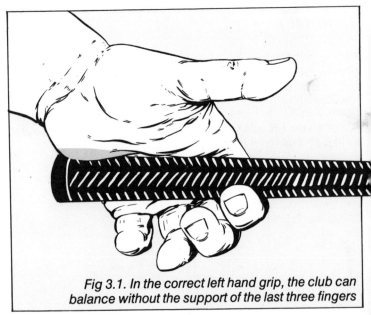

Fig 3.1. In the correct left hand grip, the club can balance without the support of the last three fingers

violently than with any other club. Unfortunately, changing the grip can be the most uncomfortable experience in golf, and there is often the temptation to stick with what *felt* right, but which in fact was wrong. But a sound grip is worth taking time over, as it contributes so much to your swing's shape and also to clubface alignment.

This chapter will teach you a grip of which you can be proud – one that will stand you in good stead as you gradually build the swing. The main purpose of the grip is to return the clubface squarely to the ball, without any unnecessary manipulation by the hands, and to allow the hands to work in harmony throughout the swing. The left hand and arm are very much the guiding and pulling force, while the right provide the extra speed and power.

Consequently, each hand is placed on the grip to allow it to work effectively. It is important to place the left hand on the grip correctly first, then apply the right, and do make sure that the leading edge of the club is square to the target.

The left hand

The club sits very much in the palm and fingers of the left hand, thus giving a more solid grip for its guiding role than if it were held only in the fingers. The club rests across the index finger and under the fleshy pad at the heel of your hand, so that it could actually be balanced in the air without the support of the last three fingers of this hand (Fig 3.1). However, these last three fingers provide the main pressure, and they should fit round the grip in such a manner that the club feels quite snug and firm. When you look down you should be able to see about two to two-and-a-half knuckles of the hand, and the 'V' formed by the thumb and forefinger should point towards your right ear, with the thumb sitting just to the right of centre of the top of the grip (Fig 3.2). Try not to let a large gap develop between the thumb and forefinger, since they need to provide a solid support at the top of the backswing. It is also a common mistake to stretch the thumb too far down the shaft. This action tenses the front of the arm and prevents the muscles from working efficiently. If you stand with your arms relaxed beside you, the end of the thumb and the knuckle of the forefinger are relatively level, and that is how you should grip the club: with the knuckle of the forefinger and the end of the thumb about level on the grip. When applying the left hand to the grip, do so with your hand opposite the inside of

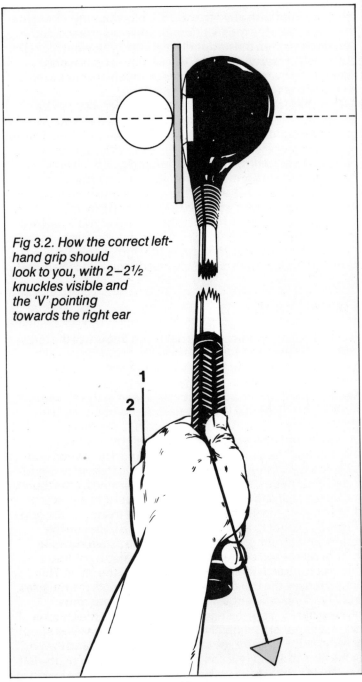

Fig 3.2. How the correct left-hand grip should look to you, with 2–2½ knuckles visible and the 'V' pointing towards the right ear

your left thigh. This will help to ensure that the shaft and clubhead are in the correct relationship to the hand and arm, i.e. virtually forming a straight line. Ensure that the back of the left hand does not become too concave, and that the shoulders are set with the left one higher than the right.

Incidentally, I do believe that it is a great help to practise taking your grip looking in a mirror, and five minutes' practice a day will quickly develop a good, comfortable grip.

The right hand

The club is gripped more in the fingers of the right hand, to encourage it to create a lively and slinging action through impact. The hollow of the palm should fit over the left thumb (Fig 3.3), so that when viewed in the mirror you can see very little of the left thumb. The 'V' formed by the thumb and forefinger, which again should not have a large gap between them, should point between the right ear and shoulder. The thumb will sit just to the left of centre on the grip, and the forefinger will be triggered at the side of the shaft (Fig 3.4). Again, as with the left hand, do not stretch the thumb down the shaft. The middle two fingers supply the main pressure, which should be sufficiently firm to control the clubhead, but not so tight that the muscles become tense.

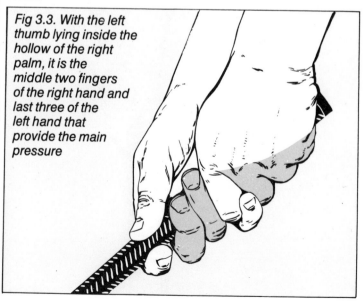

Fig 3.3. With the left thumb lying inside the hollow of the right palm, it is the middle two fingers of the right hand and last three of the left hand that provide the main pressure

THE IMPORTANCE OF THE CORRECT GRIP

Fig 3.4. The correct grip, with the triggered right forefinger, parallel 'V's and hidden left thumb

20

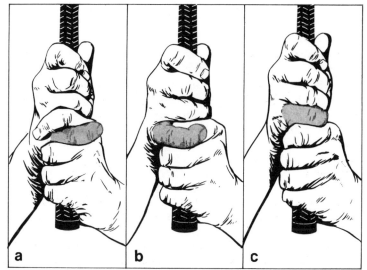

Fig 3.5. Placement of right little finger, showing: (a) interlocking; (b) overlapping or Vardon; (c) baseball or two-handed grips

What to do with the little finger

In order to make the hands work together as one unit, the right little finger is taken off the grip and either interlocked with, or allowed to overlap, the left forefinger. Most top-class players choose to overlap, and I tend to favour this, since it allows the whole of the important guiding left hand to remain on the grip. However, many players interlock, most notably Jack Nicklaus, and it does not appear to have done him any harm! He favours this grip as he has smallish hands, but many people with even smaller hands overlap, so I suggest that you adopt whichever method is most comfortable to you. Some ladies may find a two-handed grip, where all 10 fingers are on the grip, even better, but make sure that there is no gap between the two hands.

How the two hands should look

Having taken your grip, when you look in the mirror, most of your left thumb should be covered and therefore hidden from view, and the two 'V's formed by the thumb and forefinger should be parallel. If they are parallel so your hands will be also; so take your grip, then just uncurl your fingers and see if this is true. If the hands are parallel they will work in harmony – otherwise they fight each other.

Grip pressure

It is difficult to be precise about this aspect of the grip. A golfer with naturally strong hands will not need to grip the club with as much force as another player with weak hands. However, the last three fingers of the left hand and the middle two of the right provide the main support, and should only grip the club hard enough to control it. If you grip with too much pressure, the muscles in the hands and forearms will become hard and tight, and in this state they do not work efficiently. The grip will also be inclined to tighten slightly as backswing pressure is felt. Thus if you start with too tight a grip, by the time you have reached impact, your grip will be vice-like. To check the pressure, grip the club, then ask a friend to take hold of the clubhead and gently turn it from left to right. The pressure should be sufficiently tight to resist any turning of the grip in your hands. But a word of warning: I tell many more people to grip lighter, than tighter, so do not strangle the club.

Bad grips to avoid

The most common bad grip among beginners is one in which the left hand is turned too much to the left, and the

Fig 3.6. Three incorrect grips to be avoided

right hand too much to the right (Fig 3.6a). This way, both hands are too much under the grip and will prevent the wrists from working correctly throughout the swing. To correct this fault the player must move both hands more on top of the grip, and follow the guide lines in this chapter. Some players place both hands too much to the right on the grip (Fig 3.6b), and will usually hook the ball or completely block their wrist action, neither of which is acceptable in driving long distances. Again follow the guidelines in this chapter, making sure that the palms face more towards the target. As an aid, ensure that the right forefinger triggers correctly at the *side* of the shaft. The player who has both hands turned too much to the left is less common (Fig 3.6c) and is more likely to slice, and swing too upright. Neither is conducive to length. Reconstruct your grip as detailed earlier in the chapter, noting the new position of the 'V's.

What is the correct position on the grip?

As you develop good hand and arm action, so you may need to adjust your grip. The beginner is better served by a grip on the strong side of neutral, i.e. the 'V's point more towards the right shoulder, thus helping to square the clubface. Once a good action is achieved and the ball starts to draw too much, then the position can be changed slightly to a more neutral grip, where the 'V's are in the standard position described earlier.

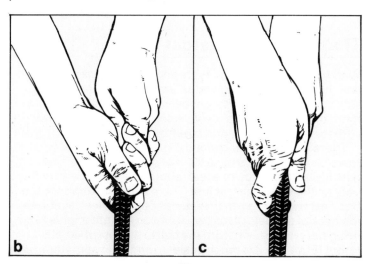

CHAPTER FOUR

How to aim and set up correctly

Nothing is more annoying than to strike the ball well, only to see it shoot off in the wrong direction. Since the driver is going to produce the longest shots in golf, it is all the more important that you aim correctly, since being out, say, 10 to 15 degrees at address, can cause a ball that travels about 200 yards to be as much as 30 to 40 yards off-line. Unfortunately, it is easy to get into bad habits and aim the shot too casually, convinced, of course, that you are firing in the correct direction. What generally happens is that to compensate for bad aiming, a swing fault is incorporated to bring the whole thing back on track. One of the most common mistakes is seeing someone who has aimed too far right, throwing the right shoulder at the ball from the top of the swing in an effort to straighten the shot. This will only prevent the correct sequence of movements from taking place in the swing, with consequent loss of power.

You must aim in the correct direction if you are trying to build sound foundations. In many sports you face your target, but in golf you are standing sideways on to your's, and several feet to the left of the intended line of flight. Also, your target may be hundreds of yards ahead, so it is easy to see why aiming the shot correctly can be such a difficult task with a combination of these factors. However, by following a set routine, you can improve this department of your game quite easily.

The intermediate target

Watch most of the best players and they adopt a routine in which instead of aiming vaguely into the distance, they select an intermediate target over which to aim, to assure them of a more precise result. Adopting this method will help to rule out sloppy and careless aiming.

Therefore you should stand behind the ball, looking towards the target, and pick out something to aim over, perhaps an old divot, or a leaf, about one yard ahead of the ball, on the ball-to-target line. Then, standing opposite the ball, feet together, with the inside of the left heel level with the back of the ball, place the clubhead at right angles to an imaginary line drawn from the ball to the intermediate target (Fig 4.1a). It is much easier to aim over something one

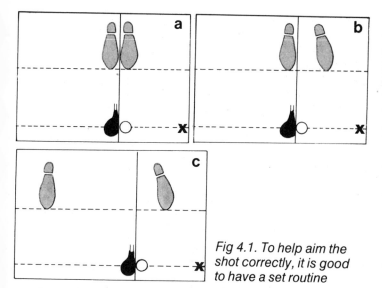

Fig 4.1. To help aim the shot correctly, it is good to have a set routine

yard away rather than 250, and with a little practice you will not find this too difficult. So having aimed the clubface correctly, now move your left foot about two inches to the left (Fig 4.1b) and the right foot a suitable distance to the right, so that the width of your stance provides a solid base on which to swing, but not one that will stifle leg action (Fig 4.1c). A line drawn across your toes should be parallel to the ball and the intermediate target line. Now make sure that your knees, hips, eyes and, most importantly, your shoulders are also parallel to this same line. The shoulders are most influential in directing the line of the swing, so do pay special attention to them.

The railway track

It will help you to aim correctly if you imagine a set of railway lines (Fig 4.2). The ball and clubhead are on the far track, and you will stand on the nearer one. That way your whole body will be parallel to the intended line of flight. So many people think that the body aims *at* the target, but if it did, the ball would start right of target. Remember that the body is aligned parallel left of the target, so that a club placed across your shoulders would point *not* at the target, but parallel left.

The best way to practise this is with two clubs on the ground to represent the railway lines. It is also useful if a

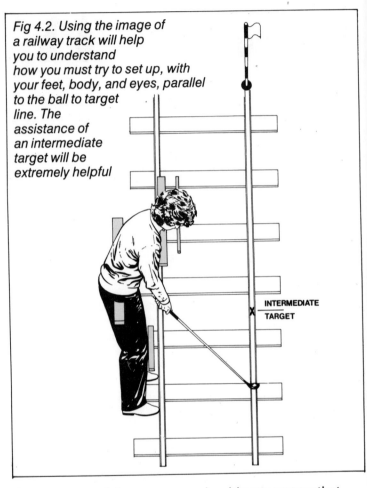

Fig 4.2. Using the image of a railway track will help you to understand how you must try to set up, with your feet, body, and eyes, parallel to the ball to target line. The assistance of an intermediate target will be extremely helpful

INTERMEDIATE
X TARGET

friend places a club across your shoulders to ensure that they are parallel, since if your aim has been wayward, the new set up will feel strange, and consequently you may interpret this as being incorrect. Any changes made in golf will often feel awkward and wrong, but this is why you must persevere and practise – otherwise, you will never improve.

The ball position

For powerful driving, you need to strike the ball when the clubhead is at the bottom of the arc or just on the way up. Position it a little nearer the left foot than for iron shots. I

26

play normal iron shots with the ball about two balls' widths inside my left heel. Therefore with the driver, the back of the ball is about one ball's width, or approximately two inches, inside my left heel. You may need to experiment to find the best position, as this will vary from player to player, but bear these facts in mind. If the ball is too far forward, it will tend to aim the shoulders left at address and will cause a weak out-to-in swing (Fig 4.3). If the ball is too far back, the shoulders will tend to point right, and you will possibly hit it while the clubhead is descending, losing distance, and will also hit it to the right (Fig 4.4). You can check the ball position by putting tee pegs in the ground to mark your toes, and one at the left heel (Fig 4.5). Place a club across the toe line, and one behind the ball. Then walk round to the other side of the ball, and see from face on just where it is. So often it appears to be in one position at address, when, in reality, it is in another. It is also extremely useful to check your set up in a mirror in which you can see the ball position easily.

Beware of the shoulder line

For powerful driving, you should play the ball nearer the left foot than for any other normal shot, and in order to

Fig 4.3. With the ball positioned too far forward, the shoulders are pulled open, i.e. aiming to the left, and the ball starts left of target

Fig 4.4. With the ball positioned too far back, the shoulders become closed, i.e. aiming too far to the right, and the ball starts right of target

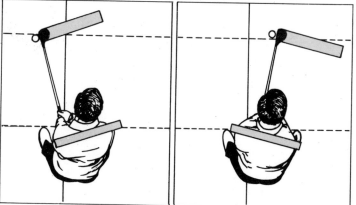

accommodate this position, it is all too easy to allow the right shoulder to be pulled forward. Instead, it should feel very much back and low, with the left shoulder feeling quite high (Fig 4.6). In the correct position, although the left arm is straight, the right elbow should be slightly bent and pointing towards the right hip bone. The left arm and shaft should form a straight line, with the back of the left hand almost level with the front of the ball.

Tailoring the stance

When driving, you use a wider stance than for any other golf shot. It is difficult to be exact about the width: too narrow,

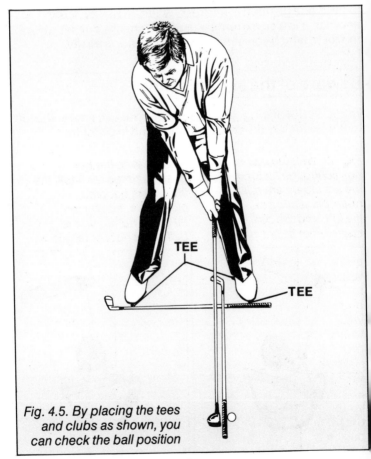

TEE

TEE

Fig. 4.5. By placing the tees and clubs as shown, you can check the ball position

Fig 4.6. Notice the line
of the shoulders
and width of feet.
The head, and fixed
pivot point are well
behind the ball, which
puts more weight on the
right side. The left arm,
which is straight,
but not stiff, forms
a line with the shaft, but
the right elbow is slightly
bent, pointing towards the hip bone

and you will not have enough stability; too wide, and you
will inhibit good leg action. It is suggested often that the
inside of the heels should be shoulder width apart (Fig 4.6)
but this will not work in practice if you have short legs and
wide shoulders, or vice versa. However, try to leave the left
foot about two inches left of the ball, and vary the width by
moving the right foot until you find the best position.

As you move your right foot to the right, you must allow
your weight to move in that direction, so that it is distributed
about 60:40 in favour of the right side (Fig 4.6). This will help
you to take the clubhead back on a shallow arc, and to strike
the ball slightly on the upswing. To help set your weight
correctly, you may find it helpful to flex your right knee a
little more than usual, which also helps to position your

head behind the ball, just where it should be at impact. Your experience now should be of looking at the back of the ball.

Most professionals position their feet so that the right is at right angles to the line of flight and the left turned slightly towards the target (Fig 4.7). The principle behind this positioning is that the right foot and leg are required to provide a stable support in the backswing, while a high degree of freedom is needed in the left leg and hip area during the through-swing. However, since we do not all have the same level of flexibility, you may find that by turning your right foot out fractionally, you can make a better backswing turn, with less strain. Certainly the older and not so slim players may find this beneficial. Again, you must experiment and find the best arrangement for support and turn on the backswing, and ease of movement on the through-swing.

The eye line

While placing your body parallel, you must also ensure that your eye line is the same. If your head is set at an angle, you will be inclined to see the line to the target incorrectly, and thus wrong messages may be fed to your brain about where you are trying to hit the ball. By holding a club across the bridge of your nose and under your eyes (Fig 4.8), you will be able to tell if they are set correctly. When looking up at the target before you hit the ball, make sure that you rotate your head in that direction, rather than lift it, which can easily offset the eye line. However, before making your backswing, it is quite in order to rotate your head slightly to the right, so that your left eye is closer to the ground than the right, thus encouraging a full turn. Many world-class players do it, so why shouldn't you?

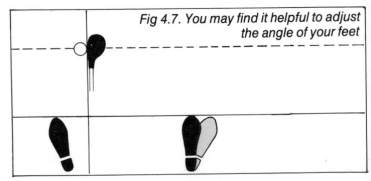

Fig 4.7. You may find it helpful to adjust the angle of your feet

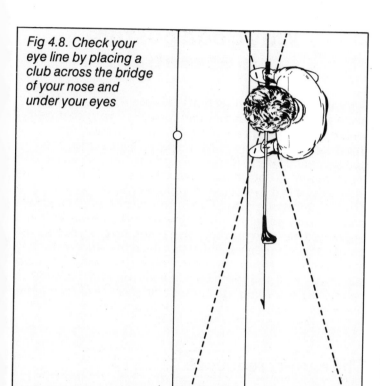

Fig 4.8. Check your eye line by placing a club across the bridge of your nose and under your eyes

How to tee the ball correctly

Since you are trying to hit the ball slightly on the upswing, it is important to guard against teeing it too low. As a good guide, the centre, or equator, of the ball should be approximately level with the top of the clubface (Fig 4.9). Usually the higher the ball is teed the higher it flies, but if you tee it too low, this may well encourage you to hit down on it and create a weak ineffectual shot.

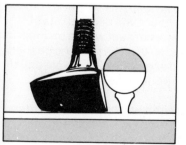

Fig 4.9. If a ball is teed correctly, the top of the club face should be about level with the equator of the ball

31

CHAPTER FIVE

Why good posture is essential

Aiming in the correct direction is essential for powerful accuracy, but it is no use aiming correctly if your posture is wrong. Many golfers are not sufficiently aware of the important role that their posture plays in the swing, and consequently how to distinguish good from bad. So let me try to enlighten you on the subject. If I had carried out all the instructions in the last chapter regarding aiming, it would be of no benefit to me if the position in which I had allowed my body and legs to settle (although parallel to the target line) prevented me from making a free swinging arm action. In a good golf swing, it is essential that the body is not in the way of the arms, and that it turns throughout the swing. The legs also play a vital and somewhat athletic role and must be positioned accordingly at address. So posture really means the way in which you angle your body and legs, and is best viewed from behind the line of flight.

The correct sequence

The correct way to gain good posture, is to stand opposite the ball with your legs straight, and then lower the clubhead to the ground behind the ball by bending from your hip bones and lowering the arms, slightly flexing your knees (Fig 5.1a). In this position, you will have a space in front of you in which your arms can swing. In fact, by bending in this fashion, the arms will hang quite freely from the shoulder joints, without the body getting in the way (Fig 5.1b). To check whether you have done this correctly, maintain your address position, take the driver in your right hand only, and hold it against your left shoulder so that the shaft hangs vertically. The clubhead should be just outside a line across your toes, although the exact amount will depend on your build. As you bend from the hips, your seat will be pushed backwards as a counter balance, so that the pelvis is pushed back and up rather than forward and under. This is essential to allow the hips to turn correctly out of the way in the backswing.

If your posture is good, the weight will be more towards the balls of your feet rather than the heels, and should be more towards the inside of each foot, with the knees slightly

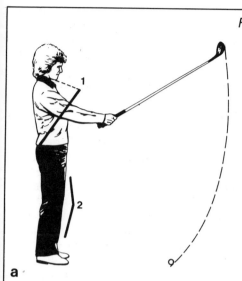

Fig 5.1a. Follow the correct sequence of movements to attain the correct posture and distance from the ball

a

Fig. 5.1b. With the back angled forward and knees flexed your arms have room in which to swing. Note that the shoulders are forward, just outside the toes

b

knocked towards each other, and the right marginally more flexed than the left. At this stage, the legs should feel in a 'lively' position, ready to support the swing. There is a theory regarding posture that you should feel as though you are just about to sit on a shooting stick. I have to disagree with this since most of your weight would be on your heels, and this is not what you require in good posture.

You also need to position your head correctly – you should hold it as an extension of the spine, in the same way as when you are standing upright. You may find, like many other golfers, that your chin is resting on your chest, often as a result of that other well misunderstood phrase: 'Keep your head down'. As you stand opposite the ball, before lowering the clubhead to the ground, fix your eyes on the horizon. Then, when taking your position, keep your head in the same relationship to your spine, just allowing your eyes to look down at the ball. Remember, head up, eyes down.

Fig 5.2a. Bad posture and ball position will inhibit a free arm swing and reduce power

Bad faults

One of the most common bad address positions is when the player's back becomes rounded and slouched, too much weight is on the heels, and the arms and hands are too close to the body (Fig 5.2a). This type of golfer would have to feel that his spine is very much straighter but angled forward at address, thus creating the desired space in which to swing. I have to admit that more women than men have bad posture, and I believe that this is partly because we are taught from an early age to try to walk erect with our backs straight and seat tucked in. Thus many women are often loath to bend sufficiently from the hips and to push their seat out. Instead, they compensate and create space in which to swing by raising their wrists (Fig 5.2b) but in so doing they prevent good hand action, so again we see one

Fig 5.2b. This posture, with the spine too erect and the wrists arched, is often adopted by ladies but should be avoided

Fig 5.2c. With the ball too far away, the legs straighten and will not work correctly to add power to the swing

fault leading to another. A woman's anatomy makes it imperative that she has her pelvis tipped back and up, since this allows the hips to turn out of the way in the backswing. In the all too familiar tucked under position, the hips get stuck in the way, and this usually results in an incorrect swaying, rather than a turning, action.

Distance from the ball

Figs 5.2a and 5.2c illustrate bad posture, allied respectively to standing too close to, and too far away from, the ball. So the distance you place between you and the ball, and your posture are inter-related. It is not possible to say exactly how far you should be from the ball, as this depends on your size, and the club length, but if your posture is correct and you take your stance as advised, you should adjust the ball position to suit this stance. One further aspect to consider is the distance between the end of the grip and your thighs. With the driver it is at its greatest (in my own case about six inches) and this helps to guarantee enough space in which to swing your arms freely. Again, it is difficult to be exact about this distance, but as a general guideline, two to three inches would be too close, and nine inches too far. It really depends on your height: taller people tending to stand closer than shorter ones. One way I have found of retaining my correct distance is to 'sight' my left forefinger knuckle against an imaginary line across my toes (Fig 5.3). In my case it appears about three inches outside this line and thus it is easy for me to see if I get too close or too far away – just by checking this measurement now and again.

Summary

Remember that the important points in good posture are to bend first from the hips, keeping the spine fairly straight and not rounded, and then flex the legs. Feel that more weight is towards the balls of the feet, and keep your head *up,* and eyes *down.*

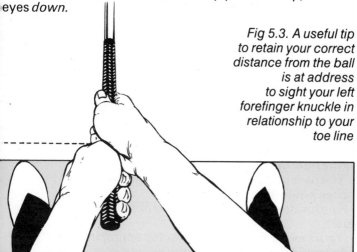

Fig 5.3. A useful tip to retain your correct distance from the ball is at address to sight your left forefinger knuckle in relationship to your toe line

CHAPTER SIX

The essential address points

The last three chapters have dealt in some depth with the most important points to consider in developing a good address position. I cannot emphasise too much the degree to which your game will improve even if you just start to look like a professional. However, do not be lulled into thinking that a good set up will happen simply by reading this book – you must practise the advice given here. The beauty of practising the address is that so much can be done at home indoors, using a mirror as your guide, or outdoors using a mirror or a long window in which you can see your reflection. It is also helpful if you have square tiles or patio slabs; otherwise, just use clubs laid down, and perhaps another golf ball as your intermediate target. By practising without the opportunity to actually hit the ball, you will concentrate better on the new position in which you will find yourself without the usual thoughts that accompany such changes: that you will never be able to hit a shot from this set up. This is a natural reaction, since anything new in golf always feels so uncomfortable, but with as little as 10 minutes' practice a day, I assure you that very soon the new set up will start to feel right, and then you will be able to concentrate on swinging the club.

So to summarize the last three chapters, and to make your mirror practice a little easier I will highlight the essential points to note.

Face on (Fig 6.1)

1 The clubface must be square to the target.
2 The two 'V's formed by the thumb and forefinger of each hand, must be parallel and pointing between the right ear and right shoulder.
3 The left thumb should be totally, or almost totally, hidden by the right hand.
4 The back of the ball should be positioned about two inches inside the left heel.
5 The inside of the heels should be *about* shoulder width apart.
6 Your weight should be distributed approximately 60:40 in favour of the right foot.

Fig 6.1. Compare your set up with the illustration shown here, going through the check lists provided in this chapter

7 The weight should favour the inside of each foot.
8 The knees should be flexed slightly towards each other, with the right a little more flexed than the left.
9 The left arm and shaft should form a straight line.
10 The left shoulder is higher than the right.
11 Your head is behind the back of the ball.

Down the target line, with the mirror to your right (Fig 6.2)

1 Your feet, knees, hips and shoulders should be parallel to the target line.
2 Although the shoulders must be parallel, because of your eye position, you should be just able to see the left shoulder.

Fig 6.2. Again, compare your set up with the position shown and refer back to the highlighted points on page 38

3 Provided that you do not alter your shoulder line, hold the club across your shoulders with your right hand, and check that the club points directly away from the mirror.

4 The right elbow should be bent a little, with the elbow joint pointing towards the hip bone so that the left arm is just visible.

5 The back should be fairly straight, not rounded, and angled forwards from the hips.

6 A line drawn down from the shoulders should be just outside a line across the toes.

7 The knees should be neither too buckled, nor too straight, but comfortably flexed.

8 Your head is still an extension of the spine, and has not been allowed to drop, so that the chin is too close to your chest (this is slightly more difficult to check, so make sure that you just *rotate* your head to the right, and not lift it).

9 There should be a suitable gap between the end of the grip and your thighs. Remember that two to three inches will be too close, whereas nine to 10 inches is too far away.

When the world's best players find that their game has lost its sharp edge, the first thing they check is their set up. Even though they play every day, their set up can still go slightly out of kilter. So please remember that if they can still check this department frequently, then you should follow suit. Once you have attained the correct address position, have rehearsed it repeatedly until it feels comfortable and one into which you can settle without a second thought, do not neglect it. Keep it in check and you will be halfway to becoming a much better golfer.

CHAPTER SEVEN

The unified swing

In Chapter 1, I stated how and where the clubhead should swing in order to produce your best drive. Now let us consider how you must move in order for this to happen. I plan to dissect the swing in order that you can have a comprehensive knowledge of its working parts. However, and I cannot emphasise this enough, golf is not a series of positions but one continuous movement, and in order to improve you have to work on specific parts of the swing in a logical order and then incorporate them into the whole movement.

It would also be fair to say that the better you become, the more finely tuned each component part of the swing has to be. You could compare it to a motor car – the average family-owned car will function even if the engine is not highly tuned, but try to drive a racing car that is not tuned correctly and you will be lucky to get out of the pit lane. The club golfer will have an enjoyable game, even with some imperfections in his swing, but he will not become a champion until they are so minute as not to cause high scores. Thus the better the component parts of the swing, the better the whole swing will become. However, do not forget that no matter how much you practise the component parts and attain different positions throughout the swing, you must work to incorporate the component parts into the whole swing – when you play and during your practice time.

As I stated earlier, golf is not a series of positions, but in teaching we have to isolate certain parts of the swing in order to highlight them, and to give you reference points. You are trying to swing the club on a certain route and if, in any part of its journey, it goes wrong, you need to be able to identify where. For example, if I was planning to travel between two places, I would pass through certain cities and towns *en route*. If I suddenly found myself in a town not mentioned on my schedule, I would know that I had gone the wrong way – this reference point would indeed warn me of my error.

So now let us take a look at the swing: first as a whole; and then in parts.

Fig 7.1. By swinging the club in a circle around a fixed point at the top of the spine, you will have a good mental picture of the golf swing

The swing image

As you stand at address, imagine swinging the clubhead on an inclined circle around a fixed point in the body, i.e. the large bone at the top of your spine and the base of your neck and you will then have a good mental picture of what happens in the correct swing (Fig 7.1). The arms will swing

Fig 7.2. The swing path of the clubhead is straight back, then inside towards 4 o'clock

6

4

the club away from the ball, and the body will turn to the right. The club is then swung down as the body turns back almost to its address position, and then the clubhead is swung up the other side as the body turns to the left. Of course, that is a highly simplistic description of what happens and does not explain in any detail how, where or when the movements are made, but nevertheless, this is the basis of what you do in the ideal swing. Let us compare that movement to the clock face analogy I used in Chapter 1.

At address, imagine a clock face, with the ball in the centre, and you positioned at 6 o'clock. As the clubhead swings away it will move towards 3 o'clock; then, as the body continues its turn and the arms swing, so the clubhead moves inwards and upwards between 3 and 4 o'clock (Fig 7.2). Ideally the clubhead is swung down on a similar path, strikes the ball as it moves towards 9 o'clock and, then swings inside towards 8 o'clock as the body continues to turn through to the target. This clock face analogy and the accompanying illustrations show you what happens in the good swing. However, in order to achieve this correct path, and depending on your swing fault, you may need to exaggerate certain movements in order to gain perfection. Please remember that the clock face system gives you, and the teacher, easier reference points to use.

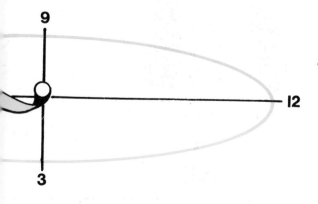

The correct way to start the backswing

So let us return to the address. As you stand there, your arms and shoulders form a triangle, with the left arm and shaft in a straight line (Fig 7.3a). As the backswing starts, you must keep that triangular relationship intact. You

Figs 7.3a. and 7.3b. By initiating the backswing with the left shoulder, arm and clubhead, you will maintain the triangle formed by the arms and shoulders at address

a

should feel that you are swinging the clubhead, left arm and shoulder away together, thus swinging that triangle to the right (Fig 7.3b). Since the pressure is applied with the last three fingers of the left hand, the muscles at the back of the left arm are brought into action as are those in the shoulder. Focus on your left side at this stage, and this will help to make sure that your body turns as your arms move, thus

b

creating a unified start to the swing. If the right hand and arm are used too actively at this point, they tend to pick the club up too abruptly, short-circuiting most of the turn required in the swing. By swinging the clubhead away with the whole of the left side, from shoulder joint to clubhead, the triangle will remain intact, and the clubhead will stay close to the ground. To the good golfer, this is a natural movement; he probably feels that if he swings his arms, then his body will respond correctly. But the high-handicap golfer and the beginner have to concentrate on ensuring that arms and body move together, so what is a conscious action for them has become ingrained and natural for the better player.

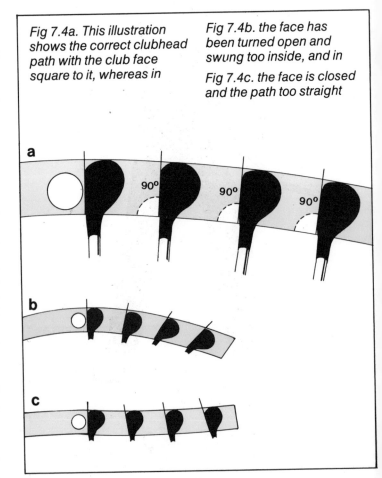

Fig 7.4a. This illustration shows the correct clubhead path with the club face square to it, whereas in

Fig 7.4b. the face has been turned open and swung too inside, and in

Fig 7.4c. the face is closed and the path too straight

The clubface

During these early stages of the backswing, there must be no manipulation of the clubhead by unwanted hand action. Indeed, the hands must feel passive at this stage, or the clubhead will be turned out of its correct path, and you will fail to achieve a shallow arc at the start of the swing. A good takeaway will see the club face remain square to the swing path, although in doing so (Fig 7.4a) it gradually starts to look right of the target. If the hands and arms turn too much to the right, the path becomes too inside, and the face rolls open (Fig 7.4b). If you interpret the takeaway as too much of a straight line, then the face may close (Fig 7.4c).

How wide should you swing the clubhead?

It is often said that width in the backswing is essential – and that is correct. However, do not imagine that if you stretch your arms away from your body as you start your backswing, that this will give you the desired width to your swing. In fact, this just puts another unwanted movement into the swing. The correct width is gained by turning your body as your arms swing. The player who fails to do this will find his body is in the way, and the arms will be forced into a steep and narrow upward swing. He may get away with this imperfection to some extent with the short irons, but not with the longer clubs, especially the driver. So to give your swing the correct width, a unified turn of the body and swing of the arms, without any undue stretching away by the arms, will provide the answer.

Leg action

Even at this early stage, the legs begin to play their part, with the left knee starting to point a little more behind the ball. Some additional pressure will be felt on the right leg, which must retain its original address position.

CHAPTER EIGHT

Checkpoints halfway back

As the swing continues from its correct start, by the time your hands reach hip height, there will be a number of points to check. Ideally, the toe of the club should point to the sky and the face should be at right angles to the horizon (Fig 8.1). Providing your grip is correct and you do not

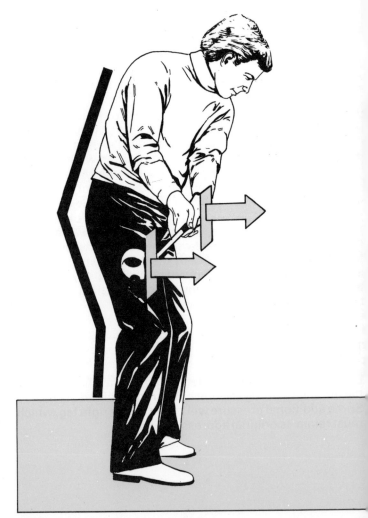

Fig 8.2. Note that the triangular
relationship of the hands and arms
still exists; the toe of the
club points to the sky, and added
pressure is being felt by the
right foot and leg

manipulate your hands independently, your arms will
rotate slightly to the right, and the back of your left hand will
face forwards. The wrists will start to cock because of the
swinging weight of the clubhead, but the hands must not
turn the club face open or closed. The triangle formation of
the arms and shoulders should still be intact, and the right
elbow will start to fold inwards and downwards. The right
hip will begin to turn out of the way, the left knee will point
more behind the ball, and there will be considerable
pressure on the right knee and inside of the leg (Fig 8.2).
While retaining the spinal angle set at address, the clubhead

Fig 8.1. The correct halfway back position
shows that the club face is at right
angles to the horizon, and the
back of the left hand faces forward.
The flex of the right knee and
angle of the spine have remained unchanged

Fig 8.3. If the hands incorrectly roll the club face open, the club face points towards the sky, and the swing path will be too much on the inside

will swing to the inside, and will be more or less in the 4 o'clock position. Remember that you are swinging around a fixed point at the base of your neck, so do not sway off the ball to the right.

If all these points are evident in the backswing, you should be able now to turn to face the club, lower the clubhead to the ground, and be back in the address position.

Positions to avoid

The two main things that can go wrong at this stage:
1 Failure to turn the body.
2 Incorrect hand action.
If these two factors are evident, either singly or combined, then you will be forced to build in compensating errors later in the swing in order to have any chance of a good and consistent strike.

Firstly, let us consider what happens when the body does not turn sufficiently. In this instance, the arms will be forced into an early upward movement, outside the desired swing path, leading to a chopping action which is exactly what you are trying to avoid. The triangular relationship of the arms and shoulders no longer exists, and therefore you have lost some of the required coordination in the swing.

The hands can work incorrectly either by turning the clubface open or closing it. If the face has been rolled open (Fig 8.3), then your hands and arms have rotated too much to the right in the backswing. Thus at hip height, the back of the left hand and clubface will not face forwards, but too much towards the sky, and the clubface will no longer be at right angles to the horizon, as in Fig. 8.1. The clubhead also will have been swung on too much of an inside path. There are two ways of getting the clubface closed on the backswing. If you keep the clubhead swinging back in a straight line for too long, the face becomes closed, as in Fig 7.4c. As the backswing progresses, the face must start to *look* open, i.e., right of the ball-to-target line, but is still square to the swing path (Fig 7.4a).

The second method of getting the club face closed is to make the backswing primarily with the right hand and arm (Fig 8.4). In this instance the club is swung inside very early,

Fig 8.4. An overactive right hand and arm have swung the club too much to the inside and have rotated anti-clockwise shutting the club face

and the wrists and arms rotate anti-clockwise. The back of the left hand becomes very *convex*, and the arms soon grind to a halt as they jam up against the right side of the body.

The correct wrist action

Perhaps the easiest way to understand how the wrists work in the swing is to perform the following exercise:

1 With your driver, stand in your address position.

2 Without moving your arms, raise the clubhead off the ground, simply by cocking your wrists straight up in front of

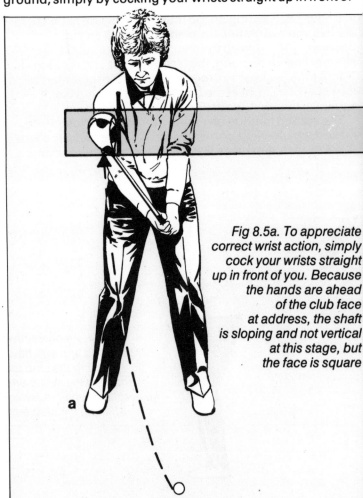

Fig 8.5a. To appreciate correct wrist action, simply cock your wrists straight up in front of you. Because the hands are ahead of the club face at address, the shaft is sloping and not vertical at this stage, but the face is square

you. Stop when the shaft is just higher than parallel to the ground (Fig 8.5a).

3 As you do so, note that the leading edge of the club does not change its angle.

This is the position the wrists should be in at about hip height. If the clubface has turned open or closed, check that your grip is not too weak nor too strong. Having carried out actions 1–3 as outlined above, turn your feet and legs 90 degrees to your left, leaving your arms and body where they were, and you will be in the correct halfway back position (Fig 8.5b).

Fig 8.5b. By turning your feet and hips to the left, leaving your arms where they were, you will be in the correct halfway back position

b

CHAPTER NINE

The best backswing position

Before I examine in detail how you should look at the end of the backswing, I want to emphasise again why teachers place such importance on this point in the swing. Go for any golf lesson and the professional will first check your set-up, and then will be most interested not only in the whole swing but also in the position you achieve at the top. This is the

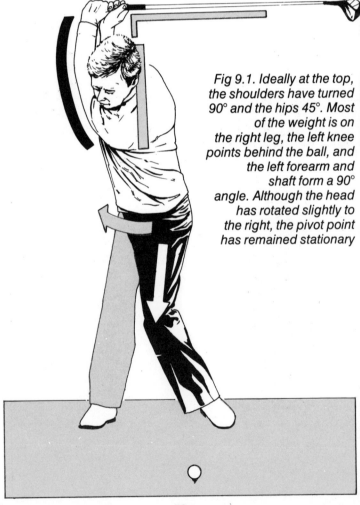

Fig 9.1. Ideally at the top, the shoulders have turned 90° and the hips 45°. Most of the weight is on the right leg, the left knee points behind the ball, and the left forearm and shaft form a 90° angle. Although the head has rotated slightly to the right, the pivot point has remained stationary

launch pad for what is to come, and if you are in a good position, then the downswing movement will become a more natural reaction. If you are way out of position at the top, you will have to make compensating errors along the way if you are to have any chance whatsoever of hitting the ball consistently.

I believe that to play golf well:

1 The better the address and set up you have, the better the backswing you will achieve.

2 The better the backswing you make, the better the downswing you will achieve.

3 The better the downswing you make, the better the strike you will achieve.

The classic position

Ideally at the top of the swing, the club shaft will be virtually parallel to the target line, and also about parallel to the ground. The club face will still be in the square position. So that tells you where the club is, but how should your body have moved to attain that position? From the correct hip height checkpoint, the shoulders *continue* turning, and the arms, dominated by the left arm, continue swinging, until the shoulders are turned approximately 90 degrees, with the hips about 45 degrees. The left shoulder will now be virtually above the right knee, which should retain about the same amount of flex as at address. Most of your weight will be resting on the right leg, with more weight directed towards the heel, but still nearer to the inside than the outside of the foot. There is, at this stage, a lot of downward pressure felt in the right leg. To facilitate this turning, the left heel may be allowed to rise slightly off the ground, but only as a last movement. The left arm, despite what is often quoted, is *not* straight, but neither is it bent into an 'L' shape. Instead it should be *slightly* bowed to prevent any unwanted tension developing. You will also notice from Fig 9.1 that the head has rotated to the right to allow a good shoulder turn, but the fixed point of the swing, near the base of the neck and top of the spine, has remained steady.

The plane of the swing

The plane of the swing is the angle at which it is inclined, and this is predetermined at address, mainly by your

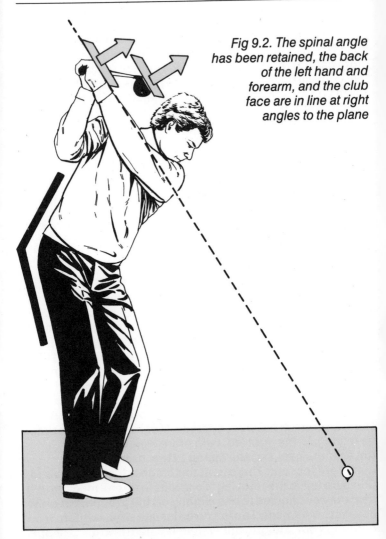

Fig 9.2. The spinal angle has been retained, the back of the left hand and forearm, and the club face are in line at right angles to the plane

posture and distance from the ball. The correct plane is found at address by extending an imaginary line upwards from the ball across the top of the shoulders. At the completion of the backswing, the left arm should lie along this line. Naturally, we cannot all afford the luxury of taking video film or photographs of our swings to check this aspect, but if you adhere to the following principles, then your plane should be acceptable:

1 Having set the spinal angle at address, do not change it – if you do, you will change the plane.

58

2 Turn your shoulders at right angles to your spine. If you stand upright and turn first to your right and then to your left, your shoulders should turn at right angles to your spine. This action is duplicated in the golf swing, with the exception that the spine is angled forward.

3 Allow your wrists to cock square to the plane as described in previous chapters.

4 Keep your elbows the same width apart throughout the backswing. If your right elbow rises too high, or gets too close to your right side, the plane will be affected.

However, as a general guideline, if you can swing your left arm into the gap between your right shoulder and your head, your swing plane will not be too far out (Fig 9.2). A short person will naturally swing his or her arms on a slightly lower plane than a tall person, so match your arm swing to your posture and build.

The hands

From the hip height position, the left wrist continues to cock upwards, (in the same direction as in Fig 8.5). Thus, at the top, it forms a 90 degree angle between the shaft and inside of the forearm. The left thumb is underneath the shaft, providing most of the support, and maximum pressure is felt in the last three fingers, which should remain firmly on the grip. The right wrist tends to be hinged back on itself, so that the palm faces half skywards. You will notice from Fig 9.2, that the back of the left hand, the forearm and clubface are in line with each other, i.e. in the same plane. If the hands had worked incorrectly, they would have turned the club face out of this good square position, which would have meant counteracting it on the downswing. That method of playing golf leads to inconsistency, since the whole swing relies too much on the small unpredictable muscles in the hands. Therefore, provided that you have a fairly neutral grip, as described earlier in the book, the clubface will be at right angles to the swing plane.

Fig 9.3a highlights how the correct clubface and wrist position should look. If the clubface is nearer right angles to the horizon (Fig 9.3b), it is open to the swing plane, and the left wrists will be excessively cupped. Fig 9.3c shows the clubface pointing towards the sky, which means it is closed to the swing plane, resulting in the back of the left wrists being convex. Whilst the wrist position in Fig 9.3a is the ideal one to achieve, it is possible, although more difficult, to play from the open position as in Fig 9.3b but more independent hand action is needed to square the club, and thus your timing has to be spot on. If you get into the closed position (Fig 9.3c), you will not be able to release the clubhead at maximum speed, thus losing distance, and you may also hook the ball violently. In the correct position, the right elbow will point to the ground. In fact, the elbows, throughout the swing, stay approximately the same width apart as at address.

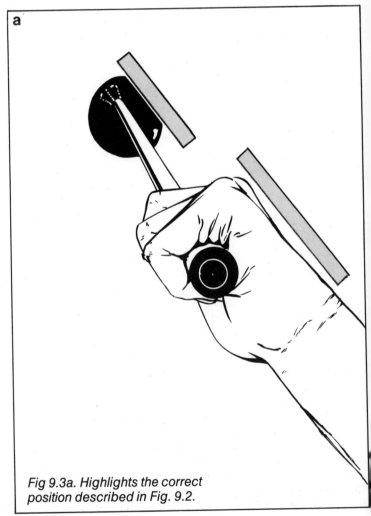

a

Fig 9.3a. Highlights the correct position described in Fig. 9.2.

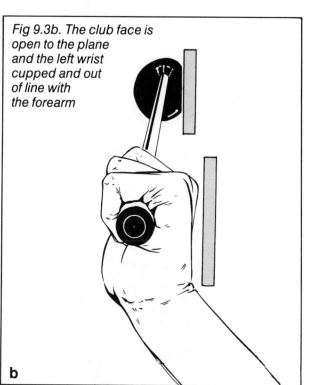

Fig 9.3b. The club face is open to the plane and the left wrist cupped and out of line with the forearm

b

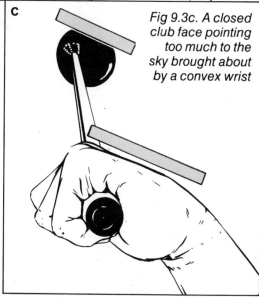

c

Fig 9.3c. A closed club face pointing too much to the sky brought about by a convex wrist

Fig 9.4. Insufficient shoulder turn results in the shaft aimed left of the target, left knee pointing ahead of the ball, and a bent left arm. A weak position – not designed for a powerful drive

The line of the shaft

The shaft should be parallel to the target line and, by and large, with most top players this is true. However, since they are often trying for additional length with the driver, due to a *greater shoulder turn* the shaft may point *slightly* right of parallel. This is acceptable, but you should not confuse their method of crossing the line with other ways of reaching the same position.

62

If you swing the clubhead too much inside at the start of the swing, i.e. directly towards 4 o'clock right from the start, then you will probably cross the line. By allowing your wrists to collapse at the top of the swing (Fig 9.3b), you will get the same result. If the shaft points left of target at the top, it could be due to taking the clubhead away more towards 2 o'clock at the start, or lack of shoulder turn (Fig 9.4).

Head still

'Keep your head still' is one of golf's favourite sayings, but it is very misleading and misunderstood. The golf club is swung around a fixed point at the top of the spine, so it is quite in order for the head to rotate to the right on the backswing, or even move to the right a *little* when driving. If you strain to keep it anchored to the spot, it may prevent the necessary weight transfer to the right side during the backswing. Thus too much weight is retained on the left side, which during the downswing will then go to the right. This is totally the reverse of what you are trying to achieve, and is called a reverse weight shift. Avoid it!

Also retain your head height, which is often lowered if a player dips the left shoulder, or raised if the same shoulder is lifted during the backswing. Swinging the arms too high can also raise the height of the head. So set your head height and maintain it.

Summary

The most important check points at the top of the backswing are as follows:

▶ shoulders turned approximately 90 degrees;
▶ hips turned approximately 45 degrees;
▶ majority of weight, about 80 per cent, on the right leg;
▶ weight retained more towards the inside and heel of the right foot;
▶ right knee still flexed;
▶ left heel just off the ground;
▶ arms swung into the slot between your right shoulder and head;
▶ left arm just slightly bowed, not straight or bent;
▶ back of the left hand, forearm and blade in line;
▶ shaft parallel to the target line;
▶ shaft virtually horizontal.

CHAPTER TEN

The downswing

During the backswing you are creating power that is used to strike the ball. However, to maximize this power, you must endeavour to swing the different parts of your body in the correct sequence in the downswing. In the backswing, your upper body and arms move before the lower half, with the left heel probably being the last part to move. This ensures that you attain a stretched feeling in your left arm and shoulder, and in the muscles down the left side of your back. You also allow the swinging weight of the club head to cock your wrists into a 90 degree angle with the left forearm creating leverage, which again is a source of power. So to swing the clubhead into the back of the ball at maximum speed, having created the power, you must store it and then use it. The best way to do this is to move your body sequentially in the right order.

The correct sequence

You could ask ten top golfers how they feel they start their downswing, and you would possibly get ten different answers. Although photography and high-speed film may well indicate that the left heel is the first part that moves, the player may not be focusing on that as his particular key to get the downswing under way. Indeed, even the top players change their ideas about how to initiate their downswing, but generally the onlooker would do well to spot any changes. Often the player may be more conscious about what a specific part of the body does at this moment in time. What happens is as follows:
▶ the left heel returns to the ground, and as it does so, the leg and hip move laterally left, transferring the weight to the left side;
▶ at the same time the left arm pulls downwards into the space created on the backswing by the right side of the body turning out of the way;
▶ the angle between the left forearm and wrist is retained in this early part of the swing, so that this power source can be used later to strike the ball (Fig 10.1).

However, problems often arise because from the top of the backswing, it is the right shoulder area that feels the more powerful, and consequently many players use that part of their body to initiate the downswing. This results in throwing the clubhead onto an unwanted outside path, from the 2 o'clock direction. You must appreciate that speed on the downswing is best provided by the arms, and then the hands, and to maximize the speed available from these two sources, the legs move in tandem with the arms, preserving that stretched feeling created in the backswing. Swing the arms correctly, and the body will follow.

Personally, I like to change direction, by moving my *left knee* towards the target, and at the *same time* I pull *down* with my *left arm,* feeling that the last three fingers of this hand are doing most of the work. This gives me a smooth change of direction, where my left hip moves laterally, my weight starts to move back to the left, and my lower and upper body move in a co-ordinated manner. It automatically enables me to retain the angle between my left forearm and the shaft, and it also keeps the club head

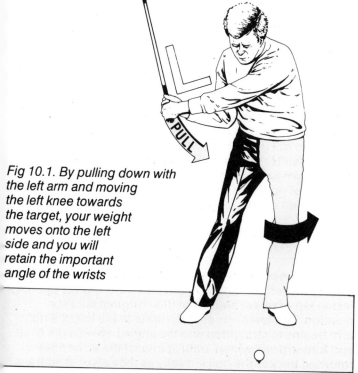

Fig 10.1. By pulling down with the left arm and moving the left knee towards the target, your weight moves onto the left side and you will retain the important angle of the wrists

Fig 10.2. By swinging your arms into the space created by turning the right side out of the way in the backswing, you will swing the club on the correct inside path.

swinging on an inside path from the 4 o'clock direction (Fig 10.2).

You may see strong men golfers employing fairly exaggerated leg action at the start of their downswing, but they match this with equally as strong hand and arm action. Do not think that by copying them you will achieve similar results. You must match leg, arm and hand action to your own particular strength. The best advice for the majority of golfers is to swing their arms down at the same time as they move their legs.

Impact zone

As the downswing progresses, the hips continue to turn back to the left, so that by impact they are slightly open, i.e. facing left of target and left of their original address position. The forearms start to rotate to the left, the right arm begins to straighten and the angle between the shaft and forearm will widen, until at impact the arms have returned back to the ball virtually as they were at address

(Fig 10.3). Whilst the backswing and change of direction are made very much with the left arm in control, the left and right hands and arms must accelerate the clubhead into the ball to get maximum speed. This is best achieved by making sure that you swing *through* the ball and not at it. So many golfers lack clubhead speed simply because they do not concentrate on swinging through the shot, and at impact the clubhead is slowing down. So as you approach impact your arms will rotate to the left, and your hands will uncock provided that you allow a free-wheeling action of the clubhead through the ball. This happens quite naturally for the better player, who allows the centrifugal force of the swing to unleash the leverage, i.e. power created between the hands and arms in the backswing. The beginner and high-handicap golfer may consciously have to think of their right hand and arm rotating towards the left, i.e. anti-clockwise, through impact, in order to square the club face (Fig 10.4).

However, the back of the left hand must not fold back on itself (Fig 10.5). It should be as it was at address, i.e. in line with the forearm, and the rotation should take place from elbow to hand.

While the arms are swinging, the legs are providing support, so that by impact you should be pushing off the instep and ball of the right foot and the heel will be starting to leave the ground. Most of the weight will be felt towards the outside of the left foot. The head and fixed point at the top of the spine, are still very steady, with the eyes focused on the back of the ball. The original spinal angle is still the same (Fig 10.2) and will continue to be so well into the follow-through. You set up with a triangular relationship between the arms and shoulders, and at impact you achieve almost exactly the same arrangement.

Fig 10.3. Impact is almost a mirror image of address. The left wrist has not buckled under the power of the right side

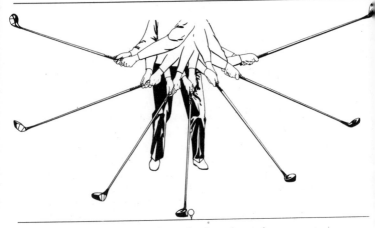

Fig 10.4. This highlights how the hands and forearms rotate anti-clockwise as they approach impact, by which time the angle between arm and shaft has straightened

The extra few yards

I think it only right to add at this point that the top-class player often chooses to draw the ball, i.e. move it from right to left for extra distance. In this instance the clubhead would be travelling more in the 4 to 10 o'clock direction, but with the club face square to the target. To draw the ball in a controlled manner, the player must have well trained hand action, and be able to swing the club on the required path. As your game develops, you can start to consider drawing the ball, but this will be when you can *consistently* swing the club down on the correct inside path, and release the clubhead at impact. Until such time as this is evident in your game, your aim should be to hit the ball consistently out of the middle of the club face, as straight as possible, at *your* maximum speed. Strive to hit it better, and you will hit it further.

The follow through

The follow through is very much a result of what has gone before in the swing, and to the trained professional eye can indicate what has happened to the shot. You will seldom see top-class players finish off balance, but go to any local club and you will notice many golfers finishing in the most bizarre fashion, totally out of control.

As the clubhead accelerates through impact, the left side, i.e. hips and body, turn out of the way to allow the hands and arms to swing through and square the club face. The right arm straightens soon after impact, and the left elbow begins to fold downwards, much as the right elbow did on the backswing. By the time the hands have reached hip height, they will be starting to cock upwards again, the back of the right hand will be facing forwards, and the toe of the club will be in the air. Whilst you may not be able to feel this happening at full pace, it is worth checking it in slow motion, and you will find that it mirrors the hip height position on the backswing. The right side of the body is pulled through so that the triangle of the arms and shoulders remains intact (Fig 10.6). Many players retard the swing by stopping the body at this point, but you should finish with your stomach either facing the target, or just to the left of it.

While the body turns, you should have the feeling of swinging your arms towards the target, in the direction of 9 o'clock. The clubhead will in fact swing back inside towards 8 o'clock because the body is turning. The same spinal angle set at address is retained, but the head starts

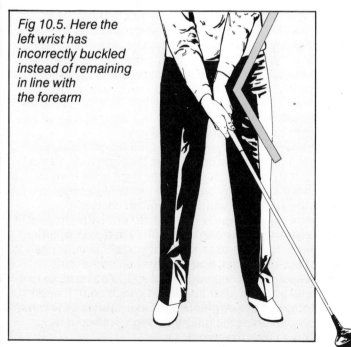

Fig 10.5. Here the left wrist has incorrectly buckled instead of remaining in line with the forearm

Fig 10.6. This halfway through position sees the toe of the club in the air and the back of the right hand facing forward, almost the reverse position to halfway back (see Fig 8.2.)

to *rotate* towards the target in order not to inhibit the follow through. As the swing finishes your arms will be in the slot between your head and left shoulder, body facing the target or left of it, most of your weight on the outside of your left foot, with the right toes being the only part of that foot in contact with the ground. You must also allow the head to move towards the target a little, so that it finishes above the left foot, with the back fairly straight (Fig 10.7) and not arched in a reverse 'C' position.

Many players deny themselves a full follow through simply because they do not release the right heel off the ground. If they felt that at impact the right knee tried to touch the left knee, they would get better leg action through the shot, and would then finish correctly.

While the spinal angle is maintained until after impact, it is permissible to allow it to rise slightly at the completion of the swing. It is also *essential* that you allow your head to rotate to face the target, and this is when you should ignore the saying: 'Keep your head still'. You must keep it steady until and just after impact, at which point it must start to rotate on the original spinal axis towards the target. At the completion of the follow through, it should be turned fully to face the target.

Fig 10.7. The head finishes almost over the left foot with the body facing the target, and perfectly balanced

Why the follow through is important

Many players find it hard to understand why the follow through is so important. As I have already said, it results from what has gone before the swing, and helps to guarantee that you accelerate through the ball. The player who becomes too ball-orientated decelerates into the shot, does not achieve maximum distance, and each swing finishes differently. This sloppy action tends to eat its way back into the swing until such time that consistent striking is a thing of the past. However, ask someone to hit the ball and hold his or her finish, and the player will swing further through the shot than before. In fact, having taught my pupils what I consider to be a decent backswing, I ask them to swing through to the finish and hold that position. By doing this, they think of swinging the club with their arms, and their hips and legs have to work more or less correctly to get them to the finish. As a professional tournament player, I prefer to leave complicated thoughts on the practice ground, and have often found that by thinking of swinging to a balanced finish, I have played my best golf.

CHAPTER ELEVEN

Timing and tempo

Once you have developed a swing that more often than not
gets the clubhead swinging down the correct 4–9 o'clock
track, it will be the timing and tempo of the swing that will
improve your distance.

Timing is the relationship of the movements between each
part of the body or, in other words, the sequence in which
the various parts move.

Tempo is the pace at which the above happens.

These two aspects of the swing are inter-related, and the
player who discovers his or her correct tempo will find
that timing of the swing will improve, and with it the
quality of strike.

Timing

The problem you face in golf is that you are using different
sets of muscles that work most efficiently at different
paces. During the backswing, many beginners feel that if
they swing their arms back and up quickly, then they will
be able to do the same on the downswing and thus hit the
ball a long way. What they fail to consider or understand is
that in order to hit the ball as far as possible, they must
give the swing the correct width and direction, and that
comes from turning the body. However, the large muscles
in the body (mainly those in the back) move slowly, whilst
those in the hands and arms move fast. The compromise is
to adopt a backswing pace, whereby you give the large
back muscles time to turn. This inevitably means slowing
down the pace of the arm swing and thinking about turning
the body.

The same problem is experienced on the downswing.
When you want to move the lower half, i.e. the legs, at the
same time as, or a little before, the arms swing down. The
large muscles in the thighs again move more slowly than
those in the hands and arms, and therefore must be given
time to contribute to the swing. Unfortunately, all too
often, from the top of the swing the player cannot wait to
'have a go' at the ball, and throws the clubhead onto an
out-to-in, i.e. 2 to 8 o'clock, path with the hands and
shoulders before any other part of the anatomy has a

Fig 11.1. Rushing the swing from the top throws the club head on to a steep out-to-in path, resulting in a pull, slice, hook, topped or skied shot

chance to respond (Fig 11.1). Whereas from the top of the backswing you want to accelerate the clubhead into the back of the ball, you must never hurry the swing at this crucial 'change of direction' stage. I always want to start the downswing at the same pace I finished the backswing, and then allow myself to accelerate the clubhead through to the finish position. In this way, I give my legs time to get the downswing under way in partnership with my arms.

The other essential timing factor involves the release of the hands. Ladies, due to possessing less innate strength than men, tend to be more guilty of throwing the clubhead with their hands from the top of the swing, thus widening that angle between the shaft and forearm too early (Fig 11.2). Before I explain how you should use your arms and hands to their greatest benefit, I must stress that I am *not* talking about hitting *late,* but about hitting at the *right* time, so that the clubhead is travelling at maximum speed at impact. During the backswing, you create power by turning your body, swinging the arms and allowing your wrists to cock under the swinging weight of the clubhead. If you start the downswing by *pulling* smoothly with the left arm

Fig 11.2. By using the hands too early, the angle between the shaft and forearms is widened, preventing this power source being used to hit the ball. The weight also remains, quite incorrectly, on the right leg

at the same time as you move the left knee towards the target, then you will retain that angle between shaft and forearm, and will be able to use that power later in the swing (Fig 10.1). By the time you strike the ball, the wrists will have fully uncocked into much the same position as at address. The problem usually results from a player thinking mainly of the hands, and not the arms swinging down.

Change direction more slowly and think of the arms swinging. Provided that you do not grip too *tightly,* the swinging weight of the clubhead will help to uncock the wrists. Beginners may have to consciously feel that the right hand and arm rotate to the left through impact, expecially if their shots are slicing. However, players who hook the ball too much usually need to speed up their leg action and check their grip.

Perfect timing is achieved on the downswing when you have co-ordinated the lower body unwinding, with:

▶ a free and uninhibited arm swing, leading to

▶ partial rotation to the left of the forearms, combined with

▶ the wrists uncocking, resulting in

▶ the clubhead swinging towards the target with a square club face at impact.

Although this may sound complicated, it will start to happen naturally once you have a reasonable idea and a picture in your mind of what should happen during the swing. Remember that in the golf swing, you create power, save power and then use power.

Tempo

You probably now realise how tempo and timing are inter-related, but sadly tempo is a much neglected part of the game. The average male beginner thinks that the faster he swings, the better the shot will be. The average female beginner tends to let herself down, not so much by swinging too fast overall because she does not have the strength, but by lacking co-ordination and timing in the downswing, and so the overall tempo is uneven.

Watch the top-class players and their swings appear to be very smooth. Some may swing faster than others, and it is always easy to appreciate the smoothness of the slower swingers, but each has found the best tempo for his or her own particular swing and stature. One way of finding your best tempo is to hit say twenty 6 irons at your usual pace, and note their average distance and spread. Then hit twenty more shots at a faster tempo, and see how these compare not only in length but also in accuracy with the original twenty. Repeat this exercise using a slower than normal pace, and again note the length and accuracy. You should be able to assess your best pace for maximum distance and accuracy. I generally tell more people to slow down rather than speed up their swing, but sometimes women have benefited by speeding up their backswing a little. This advice applies only to the woman who takes the club away so slowly that she builds no momentum or rhythm into her swing and then just lurches at the ball with the top half of her body.

I want to highlight an instance that is familiar to most golfers. On the course, you are faced with a shot from the fairway that requires your best strike with a 3 wood to carry a bunker or ditch. You decide to lay up with an iron and make a smooth, leisurely swing that sends the ball into the distance like a rocket, sometimes landing in the hazard. In that swing, your tempo and timing were perfectly matched, and yet you probably felt that you did nothing. Try using this scenario to encourage and promote good rhythm, timing and tempo.

CHAPTER TWELVE

The feel of the swing

It is difficult to be precise about how your swing should feel. Whereas 20 pupils may all be executing the same movement, each may feel the movement in a different way. I want to highlight some advice that I have found useful both as a teacher and as a professional tournament player.

1 At address, try to make your upper body as relaxed as possible, although your legs should feel a little more lively. One good way to encourage as relaxed an attitude as possible is to have a set pre-shot routine. This should start by standing behind the ball and finding your intermediate target. Address the ball and then if you usually look at the target twice, keep to that routine whatever the situation. You might like to incorporate a few waggles of the clubhead, as this action serves two purposes: it stops the muscles from getting tense; and it also programmes the initial move of the clubhead. Many players also build in some sort of trigger movement so that the swing does not start from a stationary position. Some forward press their hands, others move the right knee slightly towards the target, or maybe rotate the head a little to the right. It does not really matter what you do, but if it helps you make a smooth takeaway, then develop a trigger action. You will also find that it helps to take a deep breath and then exhale prior to making your swing.

2 The art of golf is *swinging* the golf club in a controlled manner. If you lose that control, you will also lose the opportunity of making consistently powerful golf shots. If your backswing is too fast, thereby ruining your control of the club, then you should feel that in the backswing, you are positioning the club at the top. In this way, you will become more aware of where the backswing ends and the downswing begins, and you will consequently swing in a slower and more controlled manner.

3 Make the start of the swing smooth, and it is more likely to be smooth throughout. Jerk the club away from the ball, and you will never achieve the smooth powerful swing that is necessary for long drives. It is well known that players like Jack Nicklaus and Sam Torrance hold the club just above the ground at address, as this helps them to start the backswing smoothly – give it a try.

4 As the downswing progresses, feel that your arms swing close to your right hip, and away from your left hip. This helps to encourage the correct inside swing path.

5 In golf we are trying to propel an object forward in much the same way as a javelin or a discus thrower. In each pursuit, the weight moves to the back foot as the arm is taken back and then transfers to the front foot, and the arm throws the object forwards. Golfers are often too timid to make a decent weight transference to the right side on the backswing, as they fear moving the head. What happens instead is that they do not move any weight at all and consequently hit weak shots. If you want powerful drives, then you must feel a good weight transference without getting over-concerned about slight head movement, provided that you swing round that fixed point. Pick up a stone, throw it over-arm and just note where your weight moves and where your head finishes. Now I am not saying that there is anywhere near as much movement of the head and body in the golf swing, but you must feel your weight move to the back foot, even if your head moves a *little* – it will probably rotate, rather than move, to the right. Then as you finish the swing, allow your weight to shift forwards so that your head finishes over your left foot.

6 As I have said, the change of direction from back to downswing is one of the most crucial parts of the swing, and one that is usually rushed. To help in this area, imagine a roller coaster ride as it climbs the steep track. By the time it reaches the top it has almost come to a standstill. When it moves over the summit, it starts to descend the other side quite slowly, but gradually increases in speed until, at the bottom of the slope, it is travelling at full speed. The golf swing should be considered in the same way. Then you will have the power when it matters – at impact (Fig 12.1).

7 In an effort to get distance, many golfers move themselves laterally too far to the left, and by impact are ahead of the ball. The result is often a skied shot or loss of power because they cannot release the clubhead sufficiently. From the top of the swing, try to imagine that you are hitting the ball *away* from yourself. The fixed point at the top of your spine and base of your neck will be more likely to remain still, and you will get maximum clubhead acceleration.

8 I have used the clock face as a guide to the clubhead path. You may need to tailor the 'hours' that I have used to suit your swing. In the ideal swing the club approaches the ball from between 3.30 and 4 o'clock, and moves towards 9, but since more golfers hit from out-to-in, i.e. in a 2 to 8 o'clock direction, I find that most people get the club on a better track by *feeling* that they are swinging from either 4 to 9, or even from 4 to 10. If you still start the ball left and slice it back onto the fairway, you are losing distance, so you may need to *feel* that you are swinging from 5 to 10 o'clock, ensuring that your grip is sufficiently strong, i.e. hands positioned far enough to the right on the grip, and that your arms and hands work through impact as described in Chapter 10. If you swing too much from in-to-out, then use the reverse procedure. The beauty of this clock face analogy is that you can adapt it specifically to suit your needs.

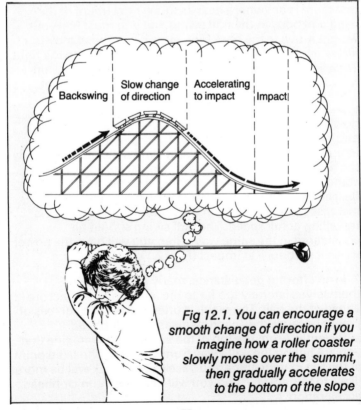

Backswing | Slow change of direction | Accelerating to impact | Impact

Fig 12.1. You can encourage a smooth change of direction if you imagine how a roller coaster slowly moves over the summit, then gradually accelerates to the bottom of the slope

CHAPTER THIRTEEN

Exercises for power

To develop your golfing muscles need not take hours each day, but if you can regularly devote just 15 minutes a day to this, then you will soon see improvements. Here are some exercises that will help to create a powerful swing.

Exercises to develop strength

1 Place a club behind your back and under your arms, and bend forwards from the hips as at address. Rotate to the right and left so that the back muscles are exercised, making a good turn easier.
2 Attach a light weight – maybe 2lbs initially – to the end of a rope attached to a piece of broom handle or something similar. Sit, with your elbows resting on your thighs, or over the back of a chair, and wind the weight up and down. This is a marvellous exercise for strengthening your forearms and hands.
3 Sit with your elbows and forearms resting on your thighs and a weight in each hand. Raise the weights up and down keeping your elbows and forearms still. Do this with your hands above and below the weights. Again, this is good for the forearm muscles.
4 Skipping is a good way to improve your hand and leg speed and will also develop your oxygen intake. However, this should be carried out only by those whose doctors would approve!
5 To improve the strength of your thigh muscles, stand with your feet apart and hands by your sides. Bend your knees, lowering yourself to the ground. Keep your weight on your toes, and your back as straight as possible. Stronger leg muscles will mean you will not tire so much towards the end of a round, and will add power to your swing more effortlessly.
6 To develop your left side, which is usually less powerful than the right, grip down the shaft of a 5 iron with just your left hand, and practise half swings. Ladies may need to support the left arm by placing the right hand, thumb uppermost, on the forearm. You must make sure that you swing as correctly as possible, so that you are ingraining the correct muscle messages. So check that halfway back the toe of the club is in the air, and the back of the left hand faces forward. Similarly, check the finish. In addition to

strengthening your muscles, the feeling of how your left hand works through impact will be heightened. You can expand on this exercise until you feel able to make a full swing; then grip at the end of the club and do it.

7 To develop all parts of the body gently, swing a weighted club, perhaps an old wood that has either had lead added inside the head (your professional will do this for you), or lead tape or something similar stuck onto the outside of the head.

8 Swinging an iron through rough is also a good exercise for strengthening hands and arms, and is more fun than cutting the grass!

9 Simply by hitting golf balls each day, you will be exercising the right muscles.

A word of warning

Do not try to do too much too soon. Start with light weights, and low repetitions. Keep a note of what you have done, and gradually build up. You will injure yourself in some way if you overdo it, and you may have to rest until the injury heals.

Exercises for technique

1 To improve hand action, using a 7 iron, make a backswing where your arms move no higher than your waist, but your wrists are almost fully cocked. Now strike the ball, creating as much clubhead speed as possible. To do this your hands have to work hard, with the right hand and forearm crossing over the left. In the backswing the end of the grip should point at the ball, and to where it was in the abbreviated follow through.

2 Insert a row of tee pegs in the ground just outside the correct backswing and downswing path, and just beyond where the ball would lie. Then practise swinging, trying not to hit the pegs. Do this without a ball and later with one.

3 Make 10 swings without the ball, concentrating on holding a balanced finish position. Then hit five shots doing exactly the same thing, and try not to let the ball inhibit you. Hold the finish to the count of five. This will develop your balance and leg action.

4 Hit six 20 irons, concentrating on your rhythm, and then hit 10 drives without letting the urge to 'have a go' ruin that rhythm. This will help you to appreciate that you do not have to throw everything at the ball to hit a drive a long way, but you must maintain your rhythm and balance.